First Facts®

National Landmarks

THE WASHINGTON MONUMENT

A 4D BOOK

by Erin Edison

PEBBLE
a capstone imprint

Download the Capstone app!

- Ask an adult to download the Capstone 4D app.
- Scan the cover and stars inside the book for additional content.

When you scan a spread, you'll find fun extra stuff
to go with this book! You can also find these things
on the web at www.capstone4D.com using the
password: wmonument.31336

First Facts are published by Pebble
1710 Roe Crest Drive, North Mankato, Minnesota 56003
www.mycapstone.com

Library of Congress Cataloging-in-Publication Data
Library of Congress Cataloging-in-Publication-Data is on file with the Library of Congress.
ISBN 978-1-5435-3133-6 (library binding)
ISBN 978-1-5435-3137-4 (paperback)
ISBN 978-1-5435-3141-1 (ebook pdf)

Editorial Credits
Erika L. Shores, editor; Sarah Bennett, designer; Eric Gohl, media researcher;
Tori Abraham, production specialist

Photo Credits
Library of Congress: 7, 11, 13, 15, 16, 17; New York Public Library: 9; Shutterstock: Gary C.
Tognoni, 19, Lindsey Zawila, 21, Patricia Hofmeester, 5, PSboom, 6, Sharp, cover; Wikimedia:
Public Domain, 4

Design Elements: Shutterstock

Printed and bound in the United States of America.
PA017

Table of Contents

The Washington Monument

The Washington Monument is an **obelisk**. This tall stone column stands on the National Mall in Washington, D.C. The mall is a long, grassy park.

This monument honors George Washington. He was the first U.S. president. Washington was also a hero during the Revolutionary War (1775–1783). He helped win freedom from Great Britain.

George Washington

obelisk—a stone column with four sides that ends in a point

George Washington died in 1799. People wanted to honor his life. Some Americans wanted a statue of Washington. Others wanted to build a **tomb** for him in the new capital city. Washington's family wanted to bury him at his farm in Virginia. The new nation would need a different way to honor their great leader.

United States of America

Washington Monument
Washington, D.C.

George Washington is buried at his home in Mount Vernon, Virginia.

tomb—a grave, room, or building that holds a dead body

The new nation's capital city was still being planned. Americans chose land between Virginia and Maryland. The capital would not be part of any state. That land is called Washington, District of Columbia. It is still the U.S. capital.

Pierre Charles L'Enfant drew the plan for the capital. The plan showed streets and buildings. It also included a spot for a monument to Washington.

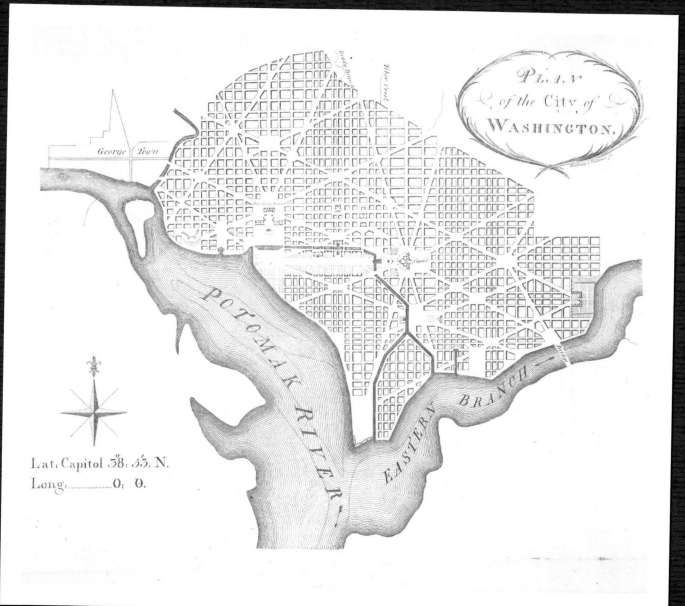

A map of L'Enfant's plans for the U.S. capital, Washington, D.C.

Designing the Monument

In 1833 the Washington National Monument Society formed. The group held a contest to find a design. **Architect** Robert Mills won the contest. His plan was to build an obelisk with columns and statues at the bottom.

The Monument Society raised money. The monument would cost $1 million. The society had only $87,000.

FACT
Robert Mills planned to build the monument 600 feet (183 meters) tall.

architect—a person who designs and draws plans for buildings, bridges, and other construction projects

A painting shows Robert Mills' idea for the Washington Monument.

Building began in 1848. By 1854 the Monument Society ran out of money. The monument was only 152 feet (46 m) tall, much shorter than planned. The society asked each state and **territory** to send stones.

A group called the Know-Nothing Party took over the plans. They fired workers who were not American. They only added 26 feet (8 m) to the monument.

FACT

The leader of the Catholic Church sent a marble block from Italy. The Know-Nothings stole it. They wanted only Americans to be involved with the monument.

territory—an area under the control of a country but not part of that country

The monument was left untouched between 1854 and 1876.

The Monument Society took over again. They still did not have enough money. The Civil War began in 1861. The project was put on hold during the war.

The war ended in 1865. Finally in 1876, the U.S. Congress took over the monument project. Congress asked the **Army Corps of Engineers** to finish building the monument. Thomas Casey was put in charge. He changed the design of the Washington Monument.

Army Corps of Engineers—a part of the U.S. Army that works on engineering projects, such as bridges and dams

This photograph of the unfinished monument was taken sometime between 1880 and 1884.

Finishing the Monument

Workers placed the final stone on December 6, 1884. President Chester A. Arthur **dedicated** the monument on February 21, 1885.

In 1888 workers put in an elevator. Now everyone could go to the top easily. The monument opened to the public on October 9, 1888.

Placing the last piece

FACT
At first, the only way to get to the top of the monument was to climb 897 steps.

A photograph from the ceremony on February 21, 1885

dedicate—to mark the official completion or opening of a building or monument

Today 50 American flags surround the Washington Monument. One flag stands for each state. In 1994 workers put a statue of George Washington in the lobby.

At times the monument has to close to the public. Workers fix it and clean it up. This allows more people to enjoy the monument safely.

FACT

In 2011 an earthquake caused more than 150 cracks in the Washington Monument. The monument closed so workers could fix the damage.

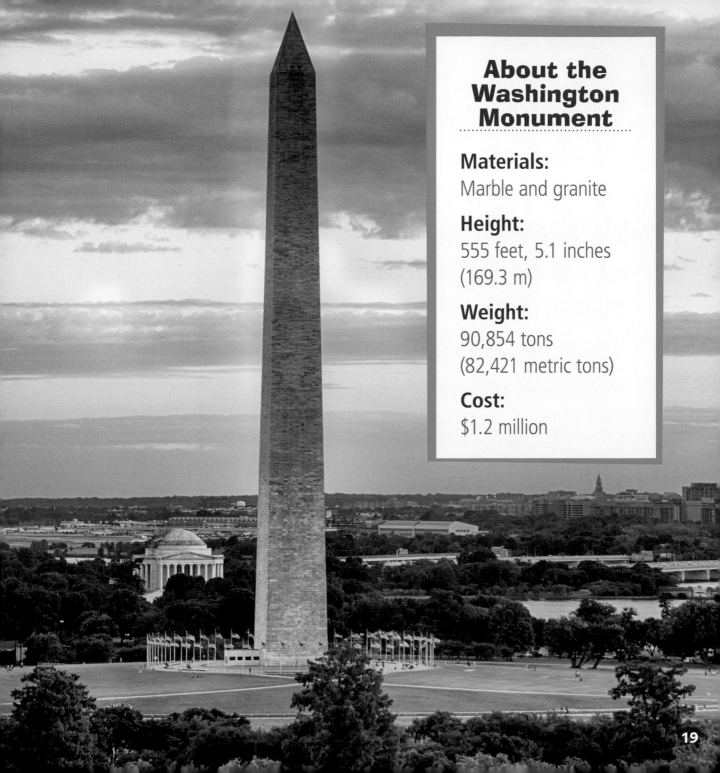

About the Washington Monument

Materials:
Marble and granite

Height:
555 feet, 5.1 inches
(169.3 m)

Weight:
90,854 tons
(82,421 metric tons)

Cost:
$1.2 million

Visiting the Monument

The Washington Monument is open all year. The National Park Service gives tours. Visitors learn the stories of the memorial stones. Visitors also take the elevator to the top. There they can see all of Washington, D.C.

Every year hundreds of thousands of visitors come to the Washington Monument. They remember the nation's first president.

Glossary

architect (AR-ki-tekt)—a person who designs and draws plans for buildings, bridges, and other construction projects

Army Corps of Engineers (AR-mee KOR of EN-gin-eers)—a part of the U.S. Army that works on engineering projects, such as bridges and dams

dedicate (DED-uh-kate)—to mark the official completion or opening of a building or monument

obelisk (OH-buh-lisk)—a stone column with four sides that ends in a point

territory (TERR-uh-tor-ee)—an area under the control of a country but not part of that country

tomb (TOOM)—a grave, room, or building that holds a dead body

Read More

Murray, Robb. *The Washington Monument: Myths, Legends, and Facts.* North Mankato, Minn.: Capstone Press, 2015.

Rawson, Katherine. *Washington Monument.* Hello, America! Minneapolis: Jump!, Inc., 2018.

Internet Sites

Use FactHound to find Internet sites related to this book.

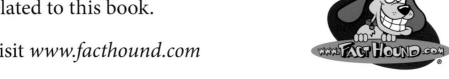

Visit *www.facthound.com*

Just type in 9781543531336 and go.

 Check out projects, games and lots more at
www.capstonekids.com

Critical Thinking Questions

1. Describe why it took so long to build the Washington Monument.

2. Why was it important for U.S. citizens to honor George Washington?

3. If you planned a new monument to George Washington, what would it look like?

Index